Ten of the Best: St[ories of] Exploration and Adventure

TEN OF THE BEST ADVENTURES IN

FROZEN LANDSCAPES

Crabtree Publishing Company
www.crabtreebooks.com

Crabtree Publishing Company
www.crabtreebooks.com
1-800-387-7650

Publishing in Canada
616 Welland Ave.
St. Catharines, ON
L2M 5V6

Published in the United States
PMB 59051, 350 Fifth Ave.
59th Floor,
New York, NY

Published in **2016 by CRABTREE PUBLISHING COMPANY.**

Printed in Canada/082019/BF20190711

Project development, design, and concept:
  David West Children's Books

Author and designer: David West

Illustrator: David West

Contributing editor: Steve Parker

Editor: Kathy Middleton

Proofreader: Rebecca Sjonger

**Production coordinator
  and Prepress technician**: Ken Wright

Print coordinator: Margaret Amy Salter

Library and Archives Canada Cataloguing in Publication

West, David, 1956-, author
        Ten of the best adventures in frozen landscapes / David West.

(Ten of the best : stories of exploration and adventure)
Includes index.
Issued in print and electronic formats.
ISBN 978-0-7787-1834-5 (bound).--
ISBN 978-0-7787-1840-6 (paperback).--ISBN 978-1-4271-7802-2 (pdf).--
ISBN 978-1-4271-7796-4 (html)

        1. Polar regions--Discovery and exploration--History--Juvenile
literature. 2. Explorers--Juvenile literature. I. Title. II. Title:
Adventures in frozen landscapes.

G580.W47 2015   j910.911   C2015-903036-6
                                                            C2015-903037-4

Library of Congress Cataloging-in-Publication Data

West, David, 1956-
 Ten of the best adventures in frozen landscapes / David West.
    pages cm. -- (Ten of the best: stories of exploration and
adventure)
 Includes index.
 ISBN 978-0-7787-1834-5 (reinforced library binding : alk. paper) --
ISBN 978-0-7787-1840-6 (pbk. : alk. paper) --
ISBN 978-1-4271-7802-2 (electronic pdf : alk. paper) --
ISBN 978-1-4271-7796-4 (electronic html : alk. paper)
 1. Arctic Regions--Discovery and exploration--Juvenile literature.
 2. Explorers--Arctic Regions--Juvenile literature. I. Title.

 G614.W47 2016
 910.911'3--dc23

                                                            2015014848

CONTENTS

Stranded in the Arctic

Willem Barentsz

In the late 1500s, European companies were making huge profits from trade with Asian countries in the Far East. Eastern spices and silks were in high demand, but European traders had to pay hefty taxes along the Silk Road—the land route to Asia. Many tried to find a different route across the top of North America. The Dutch, however, decided to look northeastward.

In 1596, Willem Barentsz was hired to search for a northeast passage to the Far East. The Dutch explorer had completed two previous expeditions to the Arctic, looking for the hoped-for passage, but both had ended in failure. Two ships set sail in May, but in July an argument between Barentsz and Van Heemskerk, the captain of the second ship, led them to separate. Van Heemskerk headed north but soon returned home after ice fields blocked his way.

Barentsz headed eastward and reached the island of Novaya Zemlya. Disaster struck when his ship became stuck fast in the ice. At first their situation did not seem too serious. They had plenty of supplies and built a strong cabin using wood from the ship. The main dangers were the cold and polar bears! One of the men chased by a polar bear escaped death only when the bear stopped to examine another bear killed earlier.

However, the Dutch sailors soon discovered that they were not equipped to deal with the savage polar winter. As ice covered the insides of the cabin and the supplies ran low, the crew survived only by trapping and eating Arctic foxes. Smoke from the fire choked the cabin, and snowfall meant they had to dig their way out. It was so cold their clothing froze on their bodies. A young cabin boy died.

In June 1597, when they realized their ship was firmly stuck, Barentsz gave orders for two smaller boats to be built. They set off as soon as they were ready. But Barentsz, who was already ill, died shortly after they left.

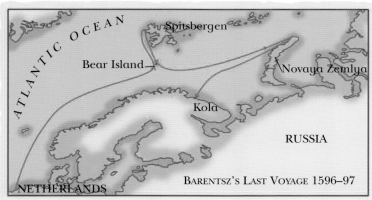

BARENTSZ'S LAST VOYAGE 1596–97

After Barentsz's death, the two boats were nearly **capsized** by a herd of walruses. Seven weeks later, they finally reached Kola in Lapland. They were lucky enough to be picked up by a passing ship. The passage was eventually found in 1878 by the Finnish-Swedish explorer Adolf Erik Nordenskiöld.

The Lost Expedition

A voyage of exploration in the Arctic, led by Captain John Franklin, left England in 1845 in an attempt to find a northwest passage to the Far East. An officer in the British Royal Navy, the 59-year-old Franklin was experienced. He had served on three previous Arctic expeditions. This particular expedition consisted of two ships—HMS *Erebus* and HMS *Terror*—and 134 men.

John Franklin

After taking on board fresh meat on the west coast of Greenland, the two ships set off across Baffin Bay. They had enough food to last them three years. Much of it was stored in tins that had been sealed with lead **solder**.

Three years later, there had been no news of the expedition. Search parties were sent out, but they failed to find any trace. In 1850, evidence of a winter camp and three graves were found on Beechey Island. In 1854, other Arctic expeditions brought back reports that 35 to 40 men had died of starvation near the mouth of the Back River, after resorting to cannibalism.

In 1859, parties set out by sled to search King William Island. They discovered a lifeboat and skeletons of crew members, as well as two messages found in a tin in a **cairn**. Dated April 25, 1848, they reported that the ships had been trapped in the ice for a year and a half. The crews had abandoned the ships on April 22. Twenty-four officers and crew had died, including Franklin, on June 11, 1847.

Many studies and searches have pieced together what happened to Franklin's lost expedition. After the ships became trapped in ice in Victoria Strait, near King William Island, many of the men died from extreme cold and lead poisoning from the tinned food and the lead pipes that provided fresh water. The remaining men headed south on foot, eventually dying from starvation and **hypothermia**. In 2014, a Canadian team discovered the underwater wreck of HMS *Erebus*.

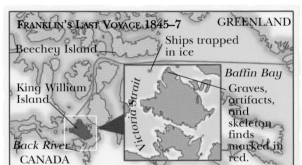

FRANKLIN'S LAST VOYAGE 1845–7 — GREENLAND — Beechey Island — King William Island — Victoria Strait — Back River — CANADA — Ships trapped in ice — Baffin Bay — Graves, artifacts, and skeleton finds marked in red.

Meeting in the Middle of Nowhere

Fridtjof Nansen

Norwegian explorer Fridtjof Nansen believed it was possible to reach the North Pole by using the natural drift of the polar ice in the Arctic Ocean. He planned an expedition to travel in a ship that was strong enough to withstand the pressures of the **pack ice**.

Aship was specially built using the toughest oak timbers. The pressure from pack ice can grip or crush a ship, so the hull of Nansen's ship was made rounder to slip upward out of the ice. Named *Fram,* which means "forward" in Norwegian, the ship left Vardø in Norway on July 21, 1893.

Following the northeast passage route, they traveled along the northern coast of Siberia in Russia until they were close to the New Siberian Islands. They headed north but, by September 20, they had become trapped in ice. The drift of the ice pack was unpredictable, sometimes even taking them south. But by January, they were moving northward at a rate of about a mile (1.6 km) a day.

Realizing it could take up to five years to reach the North Pole, Nansen and crew member Hjalmar Johansen decided to make a dash for it by dogsled.

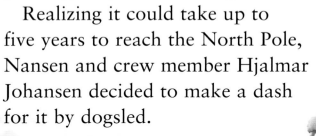

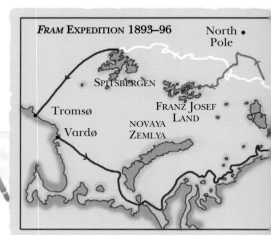

FRAM EXPEDITION 1893–96

North Pole

SPITSBERGEN

TROMSØ

FRANZ JOSEF LAND

NOVAYA ZEMLYA

VARDØ

The *Fram* would continue on its journey with the rest of the crew. On March 14, Nansen and Johansen set off, well equipped with dogsleds and kayaks. After making a good start, the pair began to find the going tough as they ran into ice block terrain. By April 7, they decided they could go no further and headed back. They had traveled farther north than any other explorer.

On their journey back both their timepieces stopped due to the cold. Without them, it was almost impossible to **navigate** accurately. By August 6, they had reached the edge of the ice and, after the last dog was killed for food, they lashed their two kayaks together and headed for the land in the distance. They reached it and Nansen decided to camp for the winter since the weather was getting colder. The pair built a hut, which served as their home for the next eight months. They shot polar bears, walruses, and seals for food and survived the Arctic winter. On May 19, not knowing where they were, they resumed their journey. Attacked at one point by walruses, they stopped to make repairs to their kayaks. Nansen suddenly heard a dog barking and went to investigate. A minute later, from out of nowhere, he saw the figure of a man.

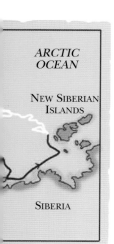

ARCTIC
OCEAN

NEW SIBERIAN
ISLANDS

SIBERIA

The man was British explorer Frederick Jackson, who was leading an expedition to Franz Josef Land. Nansen and Johansen were saved and eventually reunited with their friends on the *Fram*, which had broken free from the ice at last and sailed to Tromsø.

Andrée's Arctic Balloon Expedition

Salomon August Andrée

In 1897, the race to reach the North Pole first was still under way when Swedish balloonist Salomon August Andrée proposed a voyage by hydrogen balloon from Danskøya, Norway, to either Russia or Canada. The flight would pass over the North Pole dragging ropes to provide a form of steering. The likelihood for success was not great. His drag-rope steering technique was unproven, and his polar balloon, which had been made in Paris, leaked. Nevertheless, Andrée had convinced the Royal Swedish Academy of Sciences that he could do it.

In July 1897, Andrée and his two crewmen lifted off from Danskøya in Norway. Moving out low over the water their balloon, called "The Eagle," was pulled down by the drag ropes and almost landed in the sea. Bags of sand used as weight to keep the balloon low were quickly dumped overboard to make the basket lighter and raise it clear of the water. At the same time 1,170 pounds (531 kg) of drag rope fell off the balloon. The balloon rose to 2,300 feet (701 m), where the lower air pressure made the hydrogen gas in the balloon begin to escape quickly. Not steerable without most of the rope system, the balloon lost height as the journey continued. More weight was dropped, but the balloon became even further weighed down by rain. After 51 hours of a bumpy ride, it finally crashed into the pack ice many miles short of the Pole.

Neither the men nor the equipment was damaged. Even the camera brought to map the region from the air was undamaged. It was immediately put to use to record their daily life. Detailed records were kept. The Eagle had been well stocked with guns, snowshoes, sleds, skis, a tent, a small boat, and plenty of food. Their clothes, however, were not designed for the harsh polar environment and did not include furs. The fate of the expedition remained a mystery for the next 33 years.

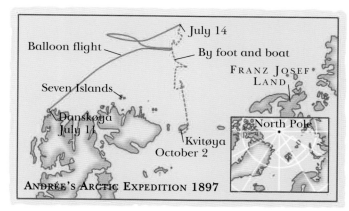

July 14
Balloon flight
By foot and boat
FRANZ JOSEF LAND
Seven Islands
Danskøya July 11
North Pole
Kvitøya October 2
ANDRÉE'S ARCTIC EXPEDITION 1897

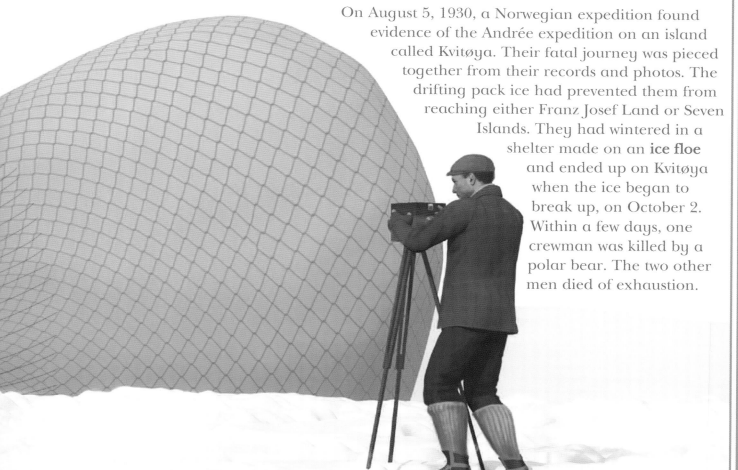

On August 5, 1930, a Norwegian expedition found evidence of the Andrée expedition on an island called Kvitøya. Their fatal journey was pieced together from their records and photos. The drifting pack ice had prevented them from reaching either Franz Josef Land or Seven Islands. They had wintered in a shelter made on an **ice floe** and ended up on Kvitøya when the ice began to break up, on October 2. Within a few days, one crewman was killed by a polar bear. The two other men died of exhaustion.

Lone Survivor

Douglas Mawson

In 1912, Australian explorer Douglas Mawson led the Australasian Antarctic Expedition to map the coastline along the Antarctic continent and collect geological samples. Traveling by sled, Mawson was part of a three-man team that included Swiss mountaineer Xavier Mertz and Belgrave Ninnis, a lieutenant in the British army.

After five weeks the party was traveling beyond a glacier (which would later be named after Ninnis), 315 miles (507 km) east of their main base camp. Mawson was on his dogsled and Mertz was on skis. Ninnis was jogging beside the second sled when he, his sled, and his dog team suddenly disappeared. They had fallen into a deep **crevasse**.

Peering over the edge, Mertz and Mawson could see two dogs on a ledge 150 feet (46 m) below—one injured and one dead. There was no sign of Ninnis. Along with their friend, they had lost their six best dogs, most of the food, their tent, and other essential supplies. After holding a memorial service for Ninnis, they headed back to base. They made a shelter out of an old tent cover held up by skis and sled runners. There was only enough food left for one week, and no food for the dogs. The men knew they would have to kill and eat their huskies one by one.

Unfortunately, the liver of a husky contains high amounts of vitamin A, which causes liver damage in humans. The men's condition rapidly deteriorated. Mertz suffered more than Mawson with diarrhea and irrational behavior. Eventually he slipped into a coma and died. Mawson buried Mertz and continued on alone. While dragging a shortened sled he, too, suddenly fell through a layer of snow and plunged into a crevasse.

Luckily, Mawson's sled acted like an anchor, and he was left dangling in midair attached by the sled harness. Using the last of his strength he managed to climb up the harness to the lip of the crevasse. But, as he climbed onto the surface, the snow gave way, and he fell back down into the crevasse. Making one last incredible effort, Mawson pulled himself up the knotted rope to safety.

Mawson eventually made it back to base camp, to find that he had missed catching a ship out by only a few hours.

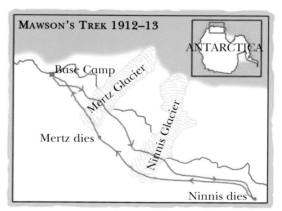

MAWSON'S TREK 1912–13

ANTARCTICA

Base Camp

Mertz Glacier

Ninnis Glacier

Mertz dies

Ninnis dies

Six men had stayed behind to search for the missing men. Mawson and the search party had to remain in the Antarctic until their ship returned ten months later.

The Last Journey

The British team at the South Pole: standing are Wilson, Scott, and Oates, sitting are Bowers and Evans.

In the race to reach the South Pole first, two teams had set off in 1911, taking different routes. Captain Robert Falcon Scott led the British expedition, called Terra Nova, and Roald Amundsen led the Norwegian expedition. The Norwegian party started from the Bay of Whales while the British set up camp on Ross Island. Both expeditions began by dropping off food and equipment along their routes. Scott was unable to get his main supply depot, called One Ton Depot, as far south as he would have liked due to tractor breakdowns and ponies unsuited to the ice.

Using dogsleds and a four-man team, Amundsen reached the South Pole on December 14, 1911. Thirty-three days later, on January 17, 1912, Scott's chosen five-man team arrived at the Pole. The temperature had dropped to -22°F (-30°C), lower than it had been when the Norwegians were there. The disappointed men took photographs and left quickly. They were suffering from slow starvation, hypothermia, and **scurvy**. On February 17, Evans slipped into a coma and died. Captain Oates was suffering terribly from frostbite. He knew he was slowing the team down. On March 17, he walked out into a blizzard saying, "I am just going outside and may be some time." It was his 32nd birthday.

The harsh weather was relentless, with blizzards making the going painfully slow for the remaining men. Finally they could go no further. Scott, Wilson, and Bowers, confined to their sleeping bags, died together in their tent— only 11 miles (18 km) from One Ton Depot.

On November 12, a search party found the tent containing the frozen bodies of Scott, Wilson, and Bowers. A cairn of snow topped with a cross was erected at the site.

Ross Island

ROSS SEA
Bay of Whales

Scott, Wilson, and Bowers died 03/29/1912

ROSS ICE SHELF

Oates died 03/17/1912

Evans died 02/17/1912

SOUTH POLE

British team 01/17/1912

Norwegian team 12/14/1911

Crean's Story

In 1911, Irish explorer Tom Crean was part of the ill-fated British Terra Nova Expedition to reach the South Pole (see pages 14–15). The journey for the British team's attempt was planned in three stages—400 miles (644 km) across the Ross Ice Shelf, 120 miles (193 km) up the Beardmore Glacier, and then a further 350 miles (563 km) to the South Pole.

Tom Crean

Crean, William Lashly, and Lieutenant Edward Evans, formed one of several teams that accompanied Captain Robert Falcon Scott on the trip to the South Pole. The plan called for only five men to travel the final leg to the Pole itself. Crean's team was not chosen. On January 4, 1912, Scott ordered them to return—a 700-mile (1,1267 km) journey back to the base camp at Hut Point.

Soon after setting out, Crean's group lost the trail back to the Beardmore Glacier. An **icefall** was the only route that led down onto the glacier. They faced a long detour if they decided to go around the dangerous icefall. With food supplies running low they decided to sled down the icefall. They hurtled out of control down the ice for 2,000 feet (610 m), barely missing massive crevasses. Their enormous risk paid off. The men reached a supply depot two days later.

By February 18, they had arrived at Corner Camp, 35 miles (56 km) from Hut Point. Their food was running low. Evans was seriously ill by then. Crean decided he should go on alone to get help. Taking only a stick of chocolate and three biscuits, Crean walked 18 hours and arrived at Hut Point in a state of utter exhaustion.

Crean had arrived ahead of a blizzard, and the rescue team was delayed for another 36 hours. Fortunately, both Lashly and Evans were brought back to Hut Point alive.

Shackleton's Rescue

Ernest Shackleton

Since the South Pole had been reached by Amundsen in 1911, there was, according to British explorer Ernest Shackleton, only one great feat of exploration left to achieve in the Antarctic—the crossing of the South Polar continent from sea to sea. Ernest Shackleton's Imperial Trans-Antarctic Expedition of 1914–17 resulted in one of the most amazing adventure stories of all time.

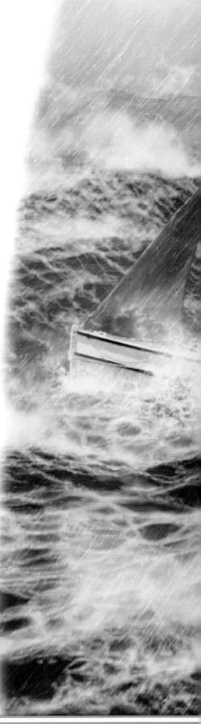

When Shackleton's ship, *Endurance*, became trapped in ice in the Weddell Sea on January 18, 1915, all hope of crossing the Antarctic was lost. The men survived the winter but, by October, they had become marooned on the ice pack when *Endurance* sank after being crushed by the ice. The 28 men of the expedition drifted on the pack ice hundreds of miles from land with no means of communication with the outside world.

The expedition camped on a flat ice floe hoping that it would drift toward Paulet Island where there were supplies. When the ice began to break up in April of the following year, Shackleton ordered the crew into the three lifeboats, and the expedition headed off across open water for Elephant Island. After five days at sea they arrived on the island, an inhospitable place far from any shipping routes. Shackleton decided to risk journeying in the open lifeboats to the **whaling stations** on South Georgia, 720 miles (1,159 km) away. One of the lifeboats was improved by raising its sides and building a makeshift deck of wood and canvas.

With enough supplies to last four weeks, Shackleton and five crew set off across the stormy Southern Ocean. After 15 days they arrived on the shores of South Georgia in the middle of a hurricane. With two of his crew, Shackleton trekked 32 miles (51 km) over treacherous mountain terrain to a whaling station. They reached the station after 36 hours—27 days after leaving Elephant Island.

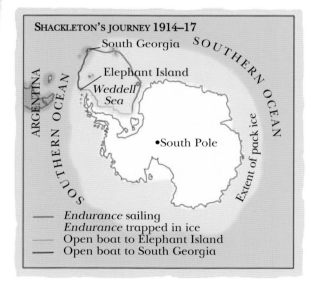

SHACKLETON'S JOURNEY 1914–17

South Georgia

SOUTHERN OCEAN

ARGENTINA

Elephant Island

Weddell Sea

SOUTHERN OCEAN

•South Pole

Extent of pack ice

—— *Endurance* sailing
—— *Endurance* trapped in ice
—— Open boat to Elephant Island
—— Open boat to South Georgia

A boat was immediately sent to pick up the three men on the other side of South Georgia. The remaining 22 men on Elephant Island were rescued four months later. Not one man from the crew of *Endurance* was lost.

Seaplanes to the Arctic

In 1925, Norwegian explorer Roald Amundsen set off to fly over the North Pole with five expedition members. Two Dornier seaplanes were used, with three men in each plane. These planes were chosen because they could land on water or ice. They were numbered N24 and N25.

Roald Amundsen

On May 21 at 5:10 pm, N25 with Amundsen and Riiser-Larsen at the controls, took off from the ice on Kings Bay, Spitsbergen, in Norway. Shortly afterward N24 followed, damaging its **fuselage** on takeoff. After eight hours, Amundsen told Riiser-Larsen to set the plane down on the ice so that they could refill the fuel tanks of both planes from the gasoline drums carried onboard N25. As the plane descended its rear engine died and they had to make an emergency landing. N24 landed some distance away, also with a failing rear engine.

Both crews set to work fixing their planes but it was soon obvious that N24 was beyond repair. On May 26, N24's crew decided to make their way to the other plane. Not far from N25, two of the crew fell through the ice. A third crew member saved them from drowning.

All six men now spent their time working to repair N25. The plane was dragged up onto the ice pack and the engine was fixed. They had managed to clear a runway on the rough ice by June 1, but the plane smashed through the ice trying to take off. A new runway now had to be laboriously cleared and smoothed with shovels and picks.

On June 15, after 500 tons (454 metric tons) of ice and snow had been moved, the runway was ready. As the Arctic summer approached, large cracks in the ice were beginning to appear. They had to leave now or never. Riiser-Larsen gunned the motors of the heavy-laden plane. The N25 hurtled down the cracked runway and lifted off into the Arctic air.

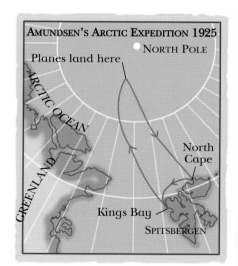

AMUNDSEN'S ARCTIC EXPEDITION 1925

NORTH POLE

Planes land here

ARCTIC OCEAN

GREENLAND

North Cape

Kings Bay

SPITSBERGEN

With fuel running low, they were lucky to make it back to Spitsbergen where they were rescued by a passing ship. The ship took them to Kings Bay where they were amazed to see the large crowd that had gathered to welcome back the aviators. Everyone had believed them to be lost forever. Amundsen went on to fly over the North Pole with Umberto Nobile in 1926, in the "Norge" **airship**.

The Italia Disaster

On April 15, 1928, the airship Italia took off from Milan, Italy, with a crew of 16 men led by Italian engineer Umberto Nobile. Nobile wanted to land men at the North Pole. *Italia* had two test flights first in Kings Bay in Norway. Then the ship headed for the North Pole on May 23.

Umberto Nobile and his dog Titina

Shortly after midnight on May 24, Italia reached the North Pole. Nobile had intended to lower scientists onto the polar ice cap, but strong winds made this impossible. Italia headed for home, but after 24 hours it had only made it halfway back. On the morning of May 25, the airship's control jammed, forcing the ship downward. The engines were stopped, allowing Italia to rise to 3,000 feet (914 m). Above the clouds, the sunshine warmed and expanded the hydrogen gas in the airship's **envelope**. This triggered valves to open, letting some of the gas out—perhaps too much.

When the engines were started again the airship descended but the tail was hanging low. Descending at two feet (61 cm) per second, Nobile realized the ship was going to hit the ice, so he ordered the engines and all electrical power to be shut down to avoid a fire. Seconds later the rear engine and the airship's cabin hit the ice and ripped open. Nine men plus Nobile and his dog were thrown onto the polar ice. Looking up, the survivors saw the airship rise again. Chief engineer Ettore Arduino threw everything he could lay his hands on down to the men on the ice. Then the airship drifted slowly away. Arduino and the other five men on board were never seen again.

Many of the survivors on the ice were injured. One man was dead. The items that Arduino had thrown to the men included food and a tent, allowing them to survive until further supplies were dropped by air. Nobile was rescued on June 23 by Swedish pilot Einar Lundborg. The last of the survivors were rescued by ship 49 days after the crash.

GREENLAND

NORTH POLE

FRANZ JOSEF LAND

Kings Bay
SPITSBERGEN

Italia crashes

ITALIA DISASTER 1928

Glossary

airship A steerable aircraft with a tube-shaped envelope filled with gas

cairn A human-made pile of stones to mark a location

capsized To turn upside down in the water

crevasse A split in ice or earth

envelope A bag that holds gas for a balloon or airship

fuselage The body of an airplane

hydrogen a gaseous element that has no color or odor and is flammable

hypothermia A condition of having a dangerously low body temperature

icefall A frozen waterfall

ice floe A sheet of floating ice

navigate To operate in a particular direction

pack ice Sea ice formed into a mass

scurvy A disease caused by a lack of vitamin C

solder A metal that is heated to join or seal the edges of a metal object

whaling station A building where whale blubber is processed into products

Index